This book is part of a project and series of centennial publications commemorating San Francisco's 1906 Earthquake and Fire. For more information on these centennial publications see:
— www.SpecialBooks.com —

Front Cover Illustration: A view down Market Street as the Call Building burns.

Illustrated with 100 half-tone Engravings from Photographs by F. E. Strohmeier, A. Blumberg, and others.
Used by permission.

Orginally Published by Leon C. Osteyee, 2010 Union Street, San Francisco, Calif.
First Printed at The Murdock Press, 1580 Geary Street, San Francisco, Calif.

The Story of the Great Disaster

San Francisco's
1906 Earthquake and Fire

By
Wilbur Gleason Zeigler

Second Edition

The Paragon Agency, Publishers
Orange, California

The Story of the Great Disaster

San Francisco's
1906 Earthquake and Fire

Zeigler, Wilbur Gleason 1857 — ?

Published by
The Paragon Agency
Orange, California
2006

1. San Francisco
2. 1906 Earthquake and Fire
3. First Person Account
4. California History
   I. Title
   II. Author

ISBN: 1-891030-63-9
Library of Congress Control Number: 2006901645

Printed in the USA
2k, r1

Preface

This is the third book in a series of republications on San Francisco's 1906 Earthquake and Fire. An authored piece, this is essentially a photographic essay on The Great Disaster. Wilbur Gleason Zeigler was born in Ohio in 1857, and grew up to be a lawyer.

He wrote only three books in his lifetime: *The Heart of the Alleghenies* (1883), *It was Marlowe* (1895), and *The Story of the Great Disaster* (1906). His book on Marlowe, was a study of the supposed author of Shakespear's writings.

There were three titles used in the original publication, as was often done in the times. Here we have selected this title because of the typical use of sensationalism.

The many publications called the event *the great disaster,* where most San Franciscans just called it The Fire. Zeigler was in San Francisco, and out from home at 5:12am on April 18th, 1906. His detailed story here could easily pass for a first person account.

We would like to thank Hank Koerper of Orange, California, for his contribution in making this republication possible.

Douglas Westfall, Publisher
January, 2006

Foreword

On Tuesday, April 17th, 1906, a business man of San Francisco ascended for the first time in five years to one of the upper stories of the highest sky-scraper in the Newspaper Angle. He was a groundling who had kept his ears as well as his feet to the earth. He was familiar with the local trade and had noted its tremendous increase; the advance of property values in like ratio; and had heard the perpetual ringing of the hammers of the artisans. On the crowded streets he felt the strong pulse of prosperity. They were symptoms of substantial growth, signs that a mighty metropolis was rearing itself upon the "hundred hills" of the peninsula; but a full vision of the thing itself, the bud unfolding into the perfect flower, had never been afforded him.

To all points of the compass, from his elevated stand, he looked with amazement and with wonder. As though the wand of a mighty architect had been waved over what had been shortly before flat roof-tops and vacant spaces of earth, between the mountains on the West and South, the hills on the North and the waters on the East, solid and imposing structures were now crowded close below him on all sides, and spotted the many hills in wide circuit,—a compact, magnificent, modern city. It seemed too splendid to be real, too substantial for illusion. He was not a dreamer, but he fancied that he saw the course of development: a natural, inevitable transformation of the remaining humble habitations into majestic edifices, of wooden shells into structures of steel,—unbroken rows along the avenues of traffic; mansions like those on Nob Hill sprinkled through the residential quarters.

In forty-eight hours the picture had changed to one of desolation. As far as the eyes of the observer had reached, and beyond the limit of his vision, spread a ruin complete and absolute, vaster then any that man had ever looked upon. The fancies of the master builders that had assumed material form and seemed of quality enduring had vanished; a mighty grave had been dug; but still, upward within the edges of the charnal-house, even before the embers were cold, the beak and then the head-feathers of the Phoenix showed, symbolical of immortality, the herald of a greater metropolis to spring from the ashes of the old.

Original Foreword of 1906

City Hall *St. Boniface Church*

Hibernia Bank *Fairmont* *St. Francis* *Market St., East* *Call Bldg.* *Hale's*

Panorama of The Business

District before the Fire.

Panorama of The Business District

from Jones Street after the Fire.

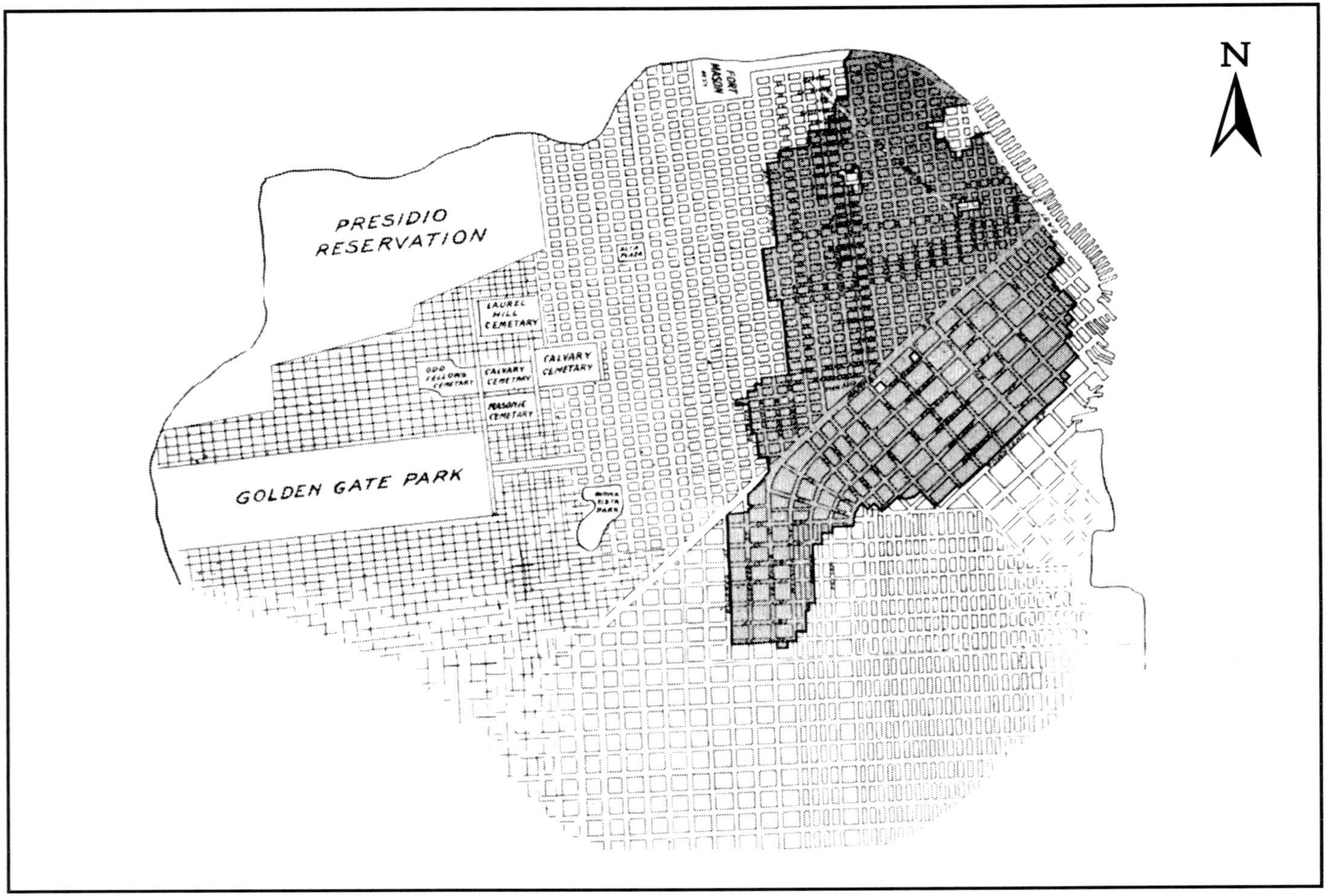

Map of San Francisco. The darker portion is the area burned, or about three-fifths of the residences of the city and the entire business section.

The Story of the Great Disaster

I left the Press Club shortly after 5 A.M. on April 18th. Only a few of the old guard were there. Just twelve hours before at a well-attended special meeting of the members, we had hotly discussed the question of a change in location. Our light had been shut off on one side by a sky-scraper, and the building of another was threatened, to further darken our quarters. The growth of the City was bringing some discomfort. There was a divided sentiment on the subject. B——, who sat with me at that early hour, was in favor of the change; I against it. As I opened the door to leave, he said jokingly;

"Only a short time more in the old quarters."

In the light of what transpired, his words seemed like prophecy.

It was an unusual hour to be out. The peace of uninhabited spaces of earth prevailed, and the dawn trembled in its firsh blush. A glow was increasing over the range culminating in Mount Diablo. I bought a newspaper from a boy and then turned down Powell Street. At the cigar stand on the next corner I stopped to get a light, and as I reached for the cord on which it suspended, I saw it swing toward me. I missed it and fell against the narrow counter, and the thought flashed through my mind that the swaying of the cord was a fancy, and that it was myself that was unsteady. I grabbed the counter and held on, realizing that the earth was shaking, and then came to me the most terrible of fears, the most sickening of sensations, like those which might be felt with the face of death close leering into your own, its icy breath upon your cheeks, its agony becoming part of you. I though of the melting of the solid flesh, and how the spark within it would pass, or was there to be absolute nothingness? My family,—I prayed only for their safety.

A tremendous and continuous crashing of glass and crystal in the drinking and dining hall almost under my feet sounded, and four men, rushing up the stone stairs, fell on their knees on the sidewalk, one praying and another begging in a maudlin voice to be told how to formulate a prayer. I recognized several prominent sporting men in the distressed group, but it did not occur to me at the time that there was anything incongruous in this exhibition.

Then came a motion that seemed the effort of an all-powerful force to loosen the firm foundation of the earth, and a thundering crash arose, as the upper part of the front of the Columbia Theater tumbled to the pavement. It resounded terrifically. The top line of the James Flood Building swayed, reached out over the street, and then swung back into place entire. It was such an uncanny phenomenon that I doubted my senses. A heavy stone step of the building within three feet of where I stood was moved out of plumb, leaving a gaping hole where it had firmly set, and almost tumbled to the pavement; open boxes of cigarettes against the wall of the stand remained in place. Later I saw a great Colonial platter, intact and still tipped carelessly and without fastenings against the walls, as it had been before the earthquake; while a heavy vase with broad base that had stood beside the platter, lay shattered on the floor. The force had worked in a manner to perplex and appall.

There was something so strange, so mysterious, so awful in its coming, presence and departure. Its approach had been like one with muffled feet in impenetrable darkness, unheralded and unsuspected; its presence manifested by an energy of destructiveness, and mischievous antics as shown in a demolishing of the apparently indestructible, a tender handling of things fragile, and a signature like the weird tracings of a freakish planchette; its passing, like that of a perturbed spirit. The odic force, displayed in all its grewsome fullness by the world mind, could not have struck greater terror in the heart of man or left a stranger trail of ruin.

The cigar dealer, with a face of frozen agitation, had jumped over or broken through the counter, and together we gained the middle of the street at the junction of Eddy, Powell and Market, and stood

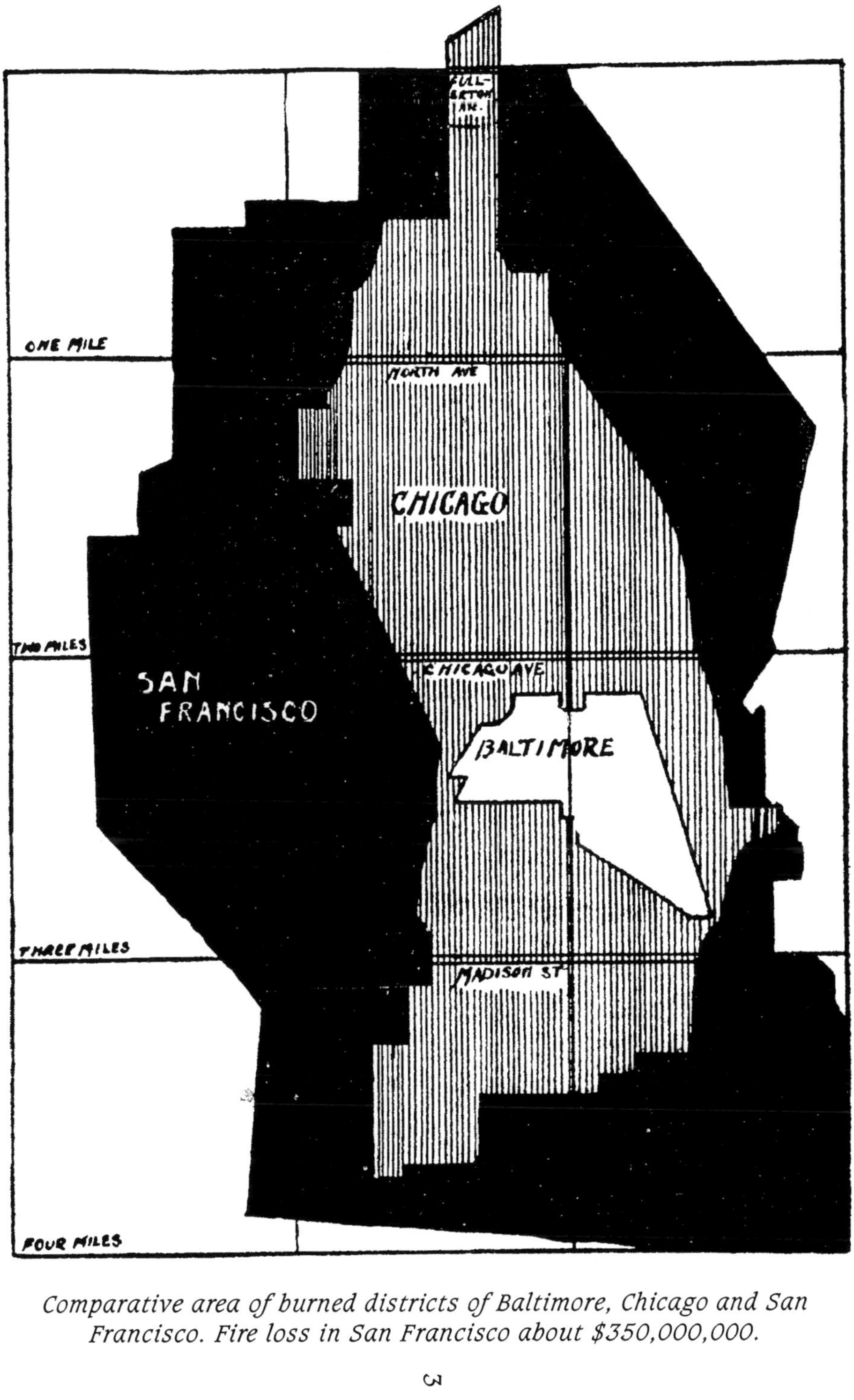

Comparative area of burned districts of Baltimore, Chicago and San Francisco. Fire loss in San Francisco about $350,000,000.

there, not daring to move in any direction. It was so still again, so peaceful! We saw the tower of the ferry house far below, like a wraithe in the soft gray light, and the upper red rim of the sun above it. The sky-pointing Call Building remained apparently unaffected by the rolling of the earth. In fact, every one of the substantial, properly built business buildings still loomed stately and unmoved upon their bases.

Someone as pale as death stretched out his hand and I shook it, recognizing an old foe. We had not spoken to one another in ten years. He said in a half-whisper:

"Wasn't that awful!"

I did not answer, but pointed to several fire-engines entering Market Street from all directions and rolling to the East and South.

"Fire," I said. "My God, how many alarms have rung?"

It happened that fifty-two were sounded in the first half-hour.

A milk-wagon passed, and I hailed the driver.

"Which way?" I asked.

"Up Market and Hayes to Fillmore."

"That's my direction for home."

"Climb up," said he.

He drew rein, and I got on the seat beside him. Then he noticed that he had lost his whip and an order book, and saying that he knew just where he had dropped them, for it was where his horses fell, he pulled them around and galloped down Market Street and into Fourth. This was to my great disgust, and against my expostulations and offers to pay for his lost articles; for my anxiety to reach home made the slightest delay unbearable. He said money would not pay for that book, or, at any rate, that he could not put a price on it, and he continued talking in this strain:

"That was a frightful shock. The horses were trotting along, when the wagon was lifted on two

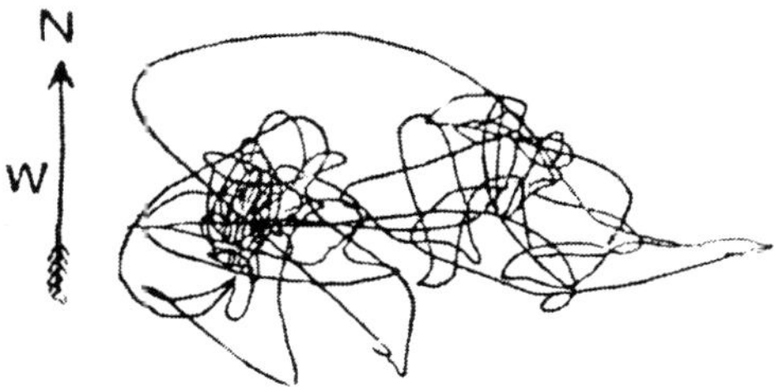

Signature of Earthquake,
April 19, 1892.

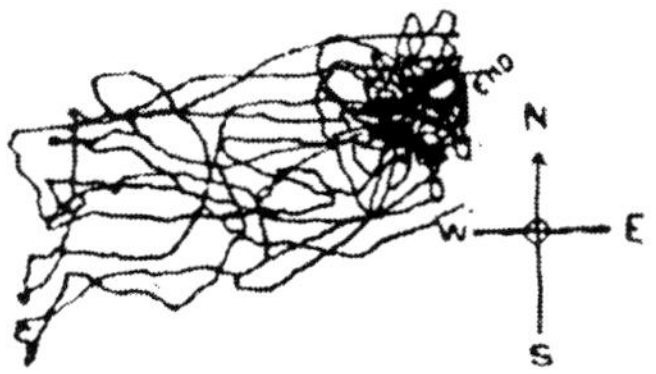

Signature of Earthquake,
April 30, 1898.

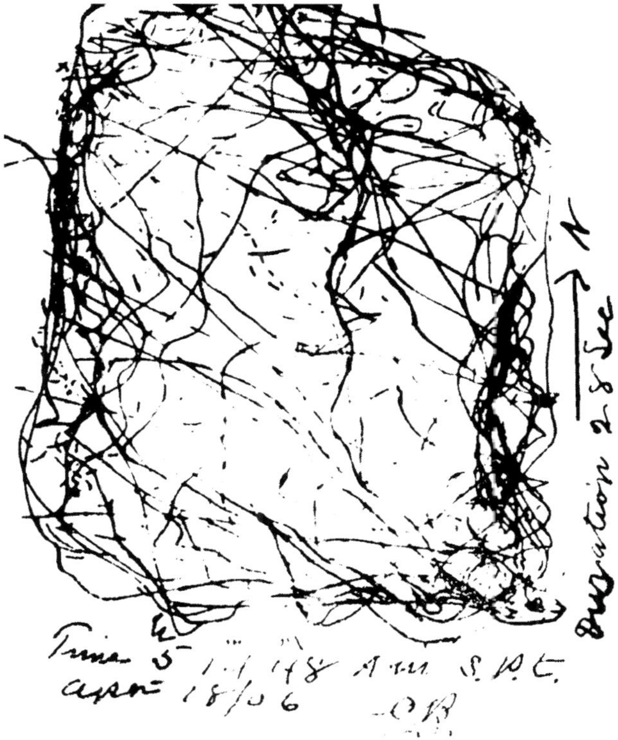

Signature of Earthquake, April 18, 1906.
"A signature like the weird tracings
of a freakish planchette."

side wheels, as though the other two had struck an obstacle. One horse fell on his knees, but jumped up immediately, and then before fifty feet had been rolled over, something seemed to strike the under side of the wagon-box like a giant trip-hammer. It was a jolt that lifted me from the seat and nearly threw me into the street, but I clung on. Both horses were thrown down, and they were trembling all over and whinnying with fright, even after I had got them on their hoofs again. I saw the surface of the street waving like a carpet with wind under it."

Several groups of men were in the middle of the streets. Some of them, half-dressed, were seated on the cable slot, putting on their shoes and stockings. Others were issuing, one by one, out of the smashed window of a restaurant, where a sagging of sills had firmly set the doors. Smoke in thin rings and streaks was curling out behind them. An excited crowd was gathered in front of a pawn shop around the corner of Jessie, some of them holding a man who it was said had just crawled out of the shop window. He had the miscellaneous contents of a showcase in a bag, and threats of hanging him were being made. The vandal was already stalking his prey. Later on, the regulars shot them down without time for prayers.

Two flimsy board structures, holding chop-houses on their lower floors, had faced each other at the corners of a narrow little street running off Fourth. Both of them had fallen outward and were heaped in a common ruin. Their dried old timbers were crossed and piled together like an upset basket of kindling. Fires were in the cook-stoves of each when they fell, and even as we stopped, held by pitiful cries from the ruin, the flames were driving back some brave men who were trying to rescue unfortunates pinned and penned in the veritable bonfire.

I had seen enough of horror, and urged the driver to turn his team. We rattled up Market Street. Affrighted people lined it, speechless, staring and apparently apprehensive of some more horrible calamity to follow. The sight of the wreck of the City Hall almost took my breath. My first glimpse of it was across Marshall Square, where still stand the monuments that portray the troublous times of early days when this spot was a wilderness of shifting sand. I looked at the rotunda. It still upheld its black dome intact, surmounted by the Goddess of Liberty; but, on the half fronting toward us, the series of ascending columns that once graced the splendid pile, and the brickwork against which they had been implanted, had been torn off, like the peel from the side of an orange. The steel ribs of a skeleton were revealed, a poverty of construction exposed; and the great building, extending its wings on all sides, was an irreparable ruin. The gigantic pillars that fronted the low, circular porch facing the avenue, had been toppled from their bases and thrown outward. They were of hollow iron, filled with concrete, mortar and bricks; and their contents and the-foliage of their capitals were scattered across the street and into the square. The rubbish before the brazen doors of this entrance was higher than the second story windows. Within, as it appeared later, the plastering of the corridors strewed the floors as completely as though barrels of cement had been exploded along them; the chandeliers were down like twisted brush-heaps; the floors of the courtrooms, offices and chambers had sunk to the basements, and the tiles of the corridors were upheaved, broken and scattered.

"How many millions gone there?" asked the practical milkman, pointing.

"Six," I said, and the thought of it staggered me; but afterward, when the fire piled up the losses to half a billion, I thought it a picayune matter.

We turned into Hayes, and at Fulton and Octavia saw a block burning. I left the wagon and went to it. Half the block was consumed before the fire was subdued, but the people on all sides treated it as a small matter, compared with the earthquake. I noticed afterward, close to the edges of the conflagration, that the householders nearest it, still guarding goods which could not be moved, appeared perfectly stolid and indifferent, while the excess of anxiety and fright was displayed by those who were many blocks from the fire.

It was well that the burnt space was placed there during the day; for its open expanse acted as a barrier to stay the greater fire of the later day and night, that spread westward from St. Ignatius

College. The use of water, even with the favorable gale, might not alone have prevented the conflagration from reaching the Park.

The civic authorities stood at their posts, conscious of the burden thrown upon them, willing and ready to bear it, and seeking through the darkness and blinding paths of the City Desolate to catch glimpses of and follow some guiding light. The order of 9 o'clock A. M. of Wednesday, placing the City under Military protection, showed how close the ear of the Mayor was to its heart-beat, how finely attuned he was to every civic vibration, and how the end inevitable must have flashed before him, even as "the king felt in his breast the phantom of the knife, long ere Ravaillac armed himself therewith."

The first order coming from Mayor Schmitz was to prevent the sale and use of liquor, and soon came the now famous order directing gas and electricity to be shut off, citizens to keep within doors after dark, to refrain from lighting fires, and stating that crime was to be suppressed by the rifle. The portion of most startling import read as follows:

"The Federal troops, the members of, the regular police force and all the special police officers, have been authorized by me to kill any person found engaged in the looting of property or in the commission of any other crime."

It was an order demanded by the occasion and the hour. It was like a command from the absolute. There was to be no parley, no hearing, no trial, no appeal. The crime—and the bullet! It bore fruit; for after the lapse of a few days not a burglary was attempted, not a robbery reported; murder was a lost art. A week after, a prominent criminal attorney said: "There is no field for me here. The only lawyer who will be engaged in the practice of criminal law is the one who for a year has been defending his own case for bigamy and perjury, and that will be his sole suit."

It was a period of peace, and Pan, the sylvan God, was almost tempted to stalk the streets.

During the fire, looters were shot down in many parts of the City, no mercy being shown where a crime was committed in the view of a soldier. In one instance a regular with a prisoner in charge appeared in the tent of a commanding officer. The prisoner was a boy, pale, trembling and callow-looking.

"Why did you bring him here?" asked the officer.

"He was caught looting."

"Why didn't you shoot him on the spot? It would have saved us the trouble of burying him."

"Well, I didn't see him looting, but the crowd did, and they pointed him out and I caught him."

"Bad work," said the officer, coolly.

The observer could not determine whether the officer was serious, or that he had spoken only to frighten the boy; but he turned away with a sickening feeling.

The same observer told me of seeing two men caught red-handed with articles of value from a store which they had entered. They were marched up the street and faced around confronting the soldiers who had them in charge. A volley of firearms rang out, and the culprits pitched forward on their faces never to rise again.

At saloons and groceries the Regulars and National Guards rolled barrels of liquor and kegs of beer out on the sidewalks and emptied their contents into the sewers.

In keeping with the violence used in the protection of property and life was the work of the brave men in rescuing unfortunates amid the ruins of the earthquake, and in the maw of the fire; in ministering to the injured, in relieving the homeless and hungry and in caring for the dead. The heroism displayed were subject for an epic; for once all men were brothers, and millionaires and paupers, the righteous and the depraved, met on terms of equality in this humane labor.

Long before noon the fire had driven out the inhabitants of the lower Mission. They trailed away in all directions, stolid sufferers carrying and dragging household goods and leading children. Some reached apparent points of safety only to be driven out later. Others, thinking the entire city was doomed, and that no place was safe outside the limits of Golden Gate Park, immediately sought its shelter. They came straggling out the streets of the Western Addition with dire tales of disaster and warnings.

"The Grand Opera House is gone," they said, "the Call Building, the Rialto; and nothing would be spared."

By noon their flight along the direct route to the park was interrupted; for a reckless woman on Hayes Street, near Market, had kindled a fire in a defective chimney, and with the destruction of her home followed a local conflagration of thirty blocks, independent of the one started directly by the earthquake. St. Ignatius Church, a million-dollar structure, was ablaze by noon, its many spires pointing like torches into the sky and its interior of treasured paintings and works of art crumbling into ashes.

Westward spread the flames, out Oak, Hayes, Grove, Fulton and McAllister Streets. They were fiercely fought by the firemen. Fortunately, an abundant supply of water was in this quarter, and the wind was soon blowing fiercely from the ocean. By night the westward progress of this fire was checked at Octavia Street; but in the meantime it had spread in the opposite direction, enveloped the Mechanics Pavilion and City Hall, and was sweeping on with uplifted lances of flame and banners of white smoke to join the like battalions from the Mission. When they met, the south line of Market Street, with all that lay close behind and far beyond it, was a smoking mass of ruins. The north line of the street was still intact, but it crumbled at the combined assault, and the flames had free course to meet those coming from the smoking region of Sansome and Post. Below the latter streets lay a rich wholesale district that, with the exception of one solidly built block, had been utterly destroyed. This block was covered by the Mills Building, the Stock Exchange, the Telephone Building, the Brooklyn Hotel, the First National Bank and many substantial wholesale houses. The fire had blistered it early in the morning, but passed on. It was now considered secure, and even the furnishings of the little hotel had been returned by six o'clock, and owners and tenants were congratulating themselves on their escape. But they counted on a false show of generosity. At nine o'clock that night the fire came back, as though it had forgotten something in its wild progress, and finished the work that it had threatened in the morning.

As the evening came on, the feeling that predominated was one of panicky fear; not of the fire, but of a repetition of the earthquake. It was held even by those who, close to the edge of the burning district, watched the progress of the flames, with all hope gone of saving their homes. That loss appeared inevitable to many; and they were resigned, for life was not threatened. But no one could foretell what would be the result of another convulsion of the crust of the earth. There would be no warning monitor, and there was no avenue of escape. Everyone realized it. As the order had gone forth prohibiting the use of lights, not even a candle was to mitigate the coming darkness behind home portals, and this increased the dread of being anywhere except in spaces open to the sky. In many districts few sought their beds. The memory of the sound of creaking and crashing beams and walls was too vivid; and so the dwellings, even far distant from the fire, were as empty of life as the tombs on Laurel Hill. Whole families, rather than trust to darkened interiors recently earthquake racked, lay on the pavements, on the doorsteps and in yards where no chimneys threatened to fall. Fortunately, the air was balmy, Nature had never been more serene, and tired women, children and men, some with no covering but their apparel, dozed on their uncomfortable resting places.

All night long the fire blazed with a splendor never equalled and a destructiveness twenty times greater than any conflagration of modern times. From a distance, we saw the Callaghan and Murphy buildings burn like builded bonfires of a hundred feet in height; the James Flood structure of twelve stories, a solid mass of flame, leaving the walls uncrumbled; the St. Francis, lifting highest its crackling crown; and through the Mission a wide wall of fire, bending and sweeping on before the wind like a living thing eager for its prey. The intonations of crashing dynamite at times came to our ears, but no, other sounds. Cinders, cold and black, fell around us at the distance of a mile from the conflagration.

Most of the men, leaving their families on their improvised beds, walked the streets, going from point to point to watch the progress and mark the course of the fire. The regulars who had been placed in charge of the city within four hours after the first tremble, paced the pavements; their signals sounding through the still air. At sight of an occasional candle in dwellings, there followed the loud pounding of the butt of a gun on the door, or the rap of a ram rod on the window, and a stentorian command to extinguish the light.

Before midnight the refugees, who had crowded into Union Square, as a place of secure encampment, were for their own salvation ordered out. Their flight was a stampede like the frightened denizens of a town before a victorious and pillaging army. Trunks and household goods, faithfully guarded during the day, were abandoned as there were no conveyances to move them, or were dragged by hand along the walks, scraping the cindered surface, sounds from their continued frequency during two days, likely to abide in memory. Women, loaded with bedding, trailed along the streets; and men, staggering with heavier burdens, pushed on for other open spaces. At the thought of losing their most treasured belongings, some grew frantic and attempted to stop the wagons loaded with goods from the stores along Kearney and Post, and use them for their own purposes. In several instances they succeeded; in others they bribed the drivers, at ten dollars a trunk, to increase their loads. The great buildings around the square, one by one catching fire, lighted up the pitiable scene.

It was the morning of the second day and a summer warmth prevailed. From Fillmore Street, which was soon to shake off its quiet and provincial air and become the principal business thoroughfare of

the changed city, I hurried down Turk to learn from personal observation what the promised. More people than usual filled the walks. There were hand-shakings as friends and acquaintances met, and some pleasant words of greeting, and again sorrow was shown over bitter experiences told. One sad group caught my attention. Women were weeping around a rabbi who was trying to comfort them, while out of one of a row of flats, down marble steps, split and shaken, a coffin was being borne toward a delivery wagon. The driver mounted his seat and drove away alone—he and the dead.

I turned from Geary into Larkin. The fire was on Leavenworth, two blocks distant. On Larkin a disturbed condition of affairs existed. The doors of many of the shops on either side of the street were wide open. Some of these groceries were entirely gutted; others had crowds before the counter and behind them. They had been opened for the pillage of the public, and the owners were aiding. Every man, returning to the sidewalk, had his arms or hands full of provisions. They continued filing in and out, some with boxes and baskets. It was a case of helping yourself to what you could without limit. I saw men looking half starved, with faces drawn and haggard, those of lost homes, and possible lost families, eating hungrily of canned goods and drinking from bottles. Women also, some with relics of finery about them, such as a treasured seal-skin coat over a shabby borrowed dress, stood there eating. A number of men were under the influence of liquor, some hopelessly so.

I reached a neighboring corner, one block nearer the fire, and there encountered a crowd at a corner grocery. The double door was locked and barred and a man in uniform, either a soldier or fireman, stood close before it. The restless crowd was clamoring to be let in, and the guardian was offering resistance. They were yelling:

"You can't save the place. Let us in. Give us the stuff instead of letting the fire get it. Break down the door."

The windows looked tempting, filled with imported goods and bottles bearing foreign labels. Someone, was forcibly pushed against the glass front. It broke; and then as the attentions of the defender of the place was turned to the demolisher, the doors gave way under pressure and the mob poured in. No further effort was made to prevent the sacking that followed; for even the man who had kept the mob at bay, said aloud, as he walked away: "The stuff would have been burned anyhow. It's better to let 'em have it."

The air was growing intensely hot; it smelled strong of fire, and cinders, warm and white-furred, fell thick upon the sidewalks. On a flight of broad steps before a mansion on the corner of Leavenworth and Geary Streets, a drunkard overcome by his potations of whiskey, slept despite the roar of the conflagration and the gruff calls of a half-intoxicated companion. The flames burst through the rear board walls of a livery stable, diagonally across the street, out of which issued the owner and hit employees, like rats deserting a sinking ship. I looked down Geary Street. It was like peering into the door of a furnace. The eyesight could penetrate but half a block, between blazing buildings lining either side, because of the concentrated white heat. One knew that the way led straight onward for more than twenty blocks through a region which could be aptly compared with nothing but hell, but devoid of the spirits of the damned.

Up Leavenworth I went to Sutter, and a block below it to the edge of the fiery mouth, I saw the square bay windows of the Pleasanton tipped and adorned with flame. A block higher up on the street I travelled, the furnishings of the Empire crowded the walks, that massive structure itself standing as though fearless of any withering touch. Nevertheless, it fell later with its cringing neighbors. The old Crocker house was as empty as though attaching creditors and loud-mouthed auctioneer had swept its floors; but its late occupants sat on its wide steps, its porches and lawns, hesitating about their exodus.

I climbed the hill to California and Hyde and glanced at the Fairmount. The demon that sent his forked tongues into the crowded haunts of the heathen, the narrow streets and alleys of Chinatown, was to be no more merciful to works modeled on the lines of Greek master-builders. That magnificent building stood like a temple inviolate, and seemingly beyond the touch of any elemental power. No one would have been disturbed as to its safety by an ordinary fire of all the encircling dwellings, separated as they were by streets on four sides; but the fury of the conflagration seemed supernatural. It must have laughed at the stolid and unconcerned aspect and attitude of that imposing pile. In fact, many attributed its burning to the torch of the incendiary; but proofs are lacking, and so was motive. The richest part of the city was to fall, and the appointed agent simply summoned the power sufficient. The Fairmount caught the sparks, nursed them for a spell and soon stood a denuded frame of discolored stone.

It was admitted that all the city from the water-front out to Van Ness Avenue was doomed. There was no salvation for it said those who marked the progress of the fire. But hope was strong for what lay beyond the bare space of one hundred and twenty-five feet that marked the avenue. There was talk of dynamite for the twenty-five continuous blocks that lined its eastern side from Vallejo to Market—two miles of splendid mansions, churches, skyscraping apartment houses, hotels, club buildings and homes endeared to those who dwelt within them, backed by the business blocks of Polk street, to be blown in air;—heroic treatment like that applied at Moscow—enough blocks, if grouped together, to make a rich city of itself. Later, the plan of clearing this richly built space of earth was modified, the situation demanding that it be carried only partly into effect by the destruction of scattered buildings in the area described.

I walked out California Street as far as Central Avenue. An unquiet feeling was prevalent through the entire distance, displayed by groups of people talking in low voices, seriously and with furtive glances to the eastern sky in which the smoke was lifted. Some were packing trunks in halls and on the porches; wagons partly filled were backed up to the walks; piles of household goods were in places heaped in readiness to be moved when the occasion demanded it. They were taking time by the forelock, anticipating the worst; and what, according to the rated speed of the conflagration, could not force them out before another day had dawned and faded.

That evening in my home quarter the neighbors fled like sheep, despite the fact that thirty burnt blocks protected it and the fire was a mile away. It was like the street of a deserted village, sans the grass, the decay, the rot of the timbers. But the air was rife with startling rumors: the fire from the Mission would climb the hills and envelope us; the wind would carry embers for miles to ignite roof tops; the efforts of the dynamiters had failed. To be alone, the sole survivor of disaster, was not to be considered for a moment. We joined the struggling caravan to higher ground, unbuilded and "open to the glimpses of the moon." Until late into the night we watched a sea of flame just beyond where the dark, unburned district terminated in the house-top line of Van Ness Avenue; this block line of spires, towers, cupolas, chimneys, flat and pointed roofs, and vacant spaces, showing against the blazing sky like the edge of a gigantic broken-toothed, cross-cut saw. We heard the frequent crash of dynamite; reports that marked brave desperate work; we saw the fire, fiercer than any that ever swept a mountains wooded side, crawl backward and up Nob Hill to destroy every landmark that had been circled in the afternoon and, in the wondrous panorama, noted the bursting of flames from every aperture of the Flood residence, which, after hours of burning, showed by its glowing windows, clearly marked, that its stone frame survived entire—an empty shell of a palace.

I missed one of the party, and found her alone near the corner of the tent crying silently in sadness and bitterness of heart—a San Franciscan weeping over loss, not in the sense of personal ownership of anything that was gone, but of the material monuments marking memories, the utter leveling and obliteration of the scenes connecting childhood, youth and womanhood. It was the display of a tender sentiment already felt, or later to be keenly experienced, by everyone whose nativity was here, I, of a distant state, could not fully comprehend or appreciate it. It is a loss restricted to the native sons and daughters.

All night the embers fell upon us as we slept, but there was no change in that marked line of housetops. The fire was greedily devouring all left within the limits to which, by the bravery and heroic endeavors of the firemen, soldiers, and civilians, it had been restricted; but, so far as the city west of Van Ness Avenue was concerned, the danger was past. Through the night we heard the call for telegraph operators to report at a stated place for duty. It sounded strangely in the still air, as though every one of them would be required to do the great work of conveying the words of a hundred thousand sufferers to distant friends. There was a free distribution from automobiles of newspapers—the combined "Call-Chronicle-Examiner"—and a rush to get them as they were scattered broadcast through the streets. All day, as of the day before, the scraping of dragged trunks over unswept pavements sounded, this time in the return to saved homes; all day the carting, packing and rolling of furniture over the streets continued. The automobiles, as on Wednesday, went without restrictions on speed, through all streets, sounding like mad things, flying from what they dreaded or speeding onward in answer to summons that brooked of no delay. There were none used for any length of time by the curious, every one as it appeared on the streets being appropriated by the civil or military authorities.

Friday found the fire confined to limits that admitted of no extension for it, except along the seawall

toward the ferry building. At three P. M. word came there to the branch postoffice that the entire water-front would soon be ablaze. Clouds of smoke from the north, drifting across the open space from which the streets converge, gave ground for the warning. The wind blew it along with increasing density. At that time the office was packed with people, sending word of their safety to distant friends. Windows were slammed down with waiting faces close against them; doors were hurriedly shut as the crowd filed out, and work for the preservation of the mail was begun. But it was not a case of the city burning to the water's edge; the fire failed in its last sally and died out before it reached the quarter threatened. And so the tower clock, that once faithful marker of the flight of time, stopped by the tremor of the earth, stares with its dead face up the broadest trail through the ruins.

It was on a hot sidewalk that the first tent was raised in the burnt district. On the next day shelters of a little more permanent character were being made with rough poles covered with scraps of sheet iron dragged from the ashes. They were the initial steps of the period of rebuilding, and taken before the conflagration had ceased burning along the sea-wall.

In the face of the calamity, there were but few who did not suppress their feelings of distress over their losses. A few days after the fire I was for several hours with an acquaintance who said nothing of his having been deprived of a monthly income of six hundred dollars, and the next day I learned of it from a mutual friend. The resolute and indomitable spirit of the age had a chance to display itself fully; and with the talk of the richer and greater San Francisco of the future, there is a union of tireless effort to realize it.

Some, possessed with the spirit of humor, displayed it like Nero fiddling over the ruins. One refugee in Jefferson Park had his tent labelled: "Well Shook," and the next one to it was "Shook Well." A curb-stone kitchen had the sign "The Outside Inn," and it looked it. A piano on a wagon bore these words: "Played on by many; the last time by a fireman." The sign of Dr. Lamb was not a hundred feet from one of Dr. Slaughter, and the passer might wonder if, for purposes other than consultation, the former might be led to the latter. "We moved because the elevator stopped running" was a notice placed on a pile of bricks—all that remained of the building formerly occupied by the man who was thus advertising. "Earthquake Shakes" was the sign above a street stand. One barber shop had this sign on its front: "Shaving. Good work; no raise;" and some wag added the letter "r" to the last word. "Quakers and

Shakers Welcome" was displayed over the door of a restaurant instead of before a gospel meeting room.

Work immediately became the order of the day. Wherever public property required clearing for travel, every man within call of the person superintending the work, or reach of his pistol, was impressed into service. On one occasion, the Secretary of State attempted to pass a body of such laborers. He was ordered to toss bricks with the other men, and he worked there until his identity was established. At a meeting of the bench and bar to devise ways and means for holding court, the question was broached as to whether exemption for the judges and their officers from such impressment should not be obtained from General Funston; but it was considered that any move to this end would be a recognition of the military power over the civil and was to be avoided.

The opportunity to make the most of what Nature has liberally provided in the way of sublime surroundings and harbor unequalled has been fully recognized, and a project for the "city beautiful" developed. A congested growth of sky-scrapers is no longer probable; for the area for business purposes has widened and the retail and wholesale districts been divided. Homes with wide-spreading lawns, hotels with spaces for out-door entertainment, parks for recreation and broad avenues, will grace and adorn the levels and the hills where dwellings and business buildings were once crowded together close to the edges of the walks.

Observatory, Strawberry Hill, Golden Gate Park, San Francisco, Damaged by Earthquake.

Nob Hill, from Sutter Street and Grant Avenue, before the Fire.

Nob Hill, North from St. Mary's Cathedral, after the Fire. Van Ness Avenue Bread Line in the foreground.

Fire about the United States Mint, Fifth Street.

The Mint, San Francisco—Withstood both Earthquake and Fire with scarcely any Damage.

Y. M. C. A. Building, Mason and Ellis Streets, after the Fire.

The Burned District as seen from Rincon Hill, San Francisco.

Chinese Joss House before the Fire.

Looking North on Sansome Street, from Bush Street, San Francisco, after the Fire.

The Wrecking of the Pacific Mutual Life Insurance Building, Montgomery Street.

Turk and Market Streets, San Francisco, after the Fire.

Valencia Street Hotel before the Earthquake.

Valencia Street Four-Story Hotel Destroyed by Earthquake. Thirty People Killed.

Looking down California Street after the Fire.

Looking down Market Street, from Eleventh Street, after the Fire.

The New Postoffice, San Francisco—did not suspend business except for a few hours to fight fire. Grant Building at left.

Jefferson Square Camp of Refugees.

Ruins of the Grand Opera House. Destroyed by Fire.

Result of Earthquake on Mission Street, opposite Postoffice.

Russian Hill, showing Houses Saved from Fire.

Break in the Street near Water Front, caused by Earthquake.

Mission District after the Fire—showing unburned portion, looking from Ashbury Heights.

The Kohl Building, California and Montgomery Streets. Withstood both Fire and Earthquake and used as Headquarters by Commanding Officers of Military.

Central Bank, Fourteenth and Broadway, Oakland.

The Mission District Burning, as seen from Market Street, near Dolores Street.

Jewish Synagogue, Sutter Street, between Powell and Stockton.

Lincoln School, Fifth Street. Damaged by Fire.

Looking down Market Street from Jones Street during the Labor Day Parade. September, 1905.

Labor Day Parade, September 3, 1906, looking North on Van Ness Avenue; 20,000 men in line.

City Hall before the Fire and Earthquake.

City Hall, San Francisco, Damaged by Earthquake.

Hall of Justice before the Fire.

Hall of Justice, San Francisco, Damaged by Fire—Showing Refugees Camped in Front.

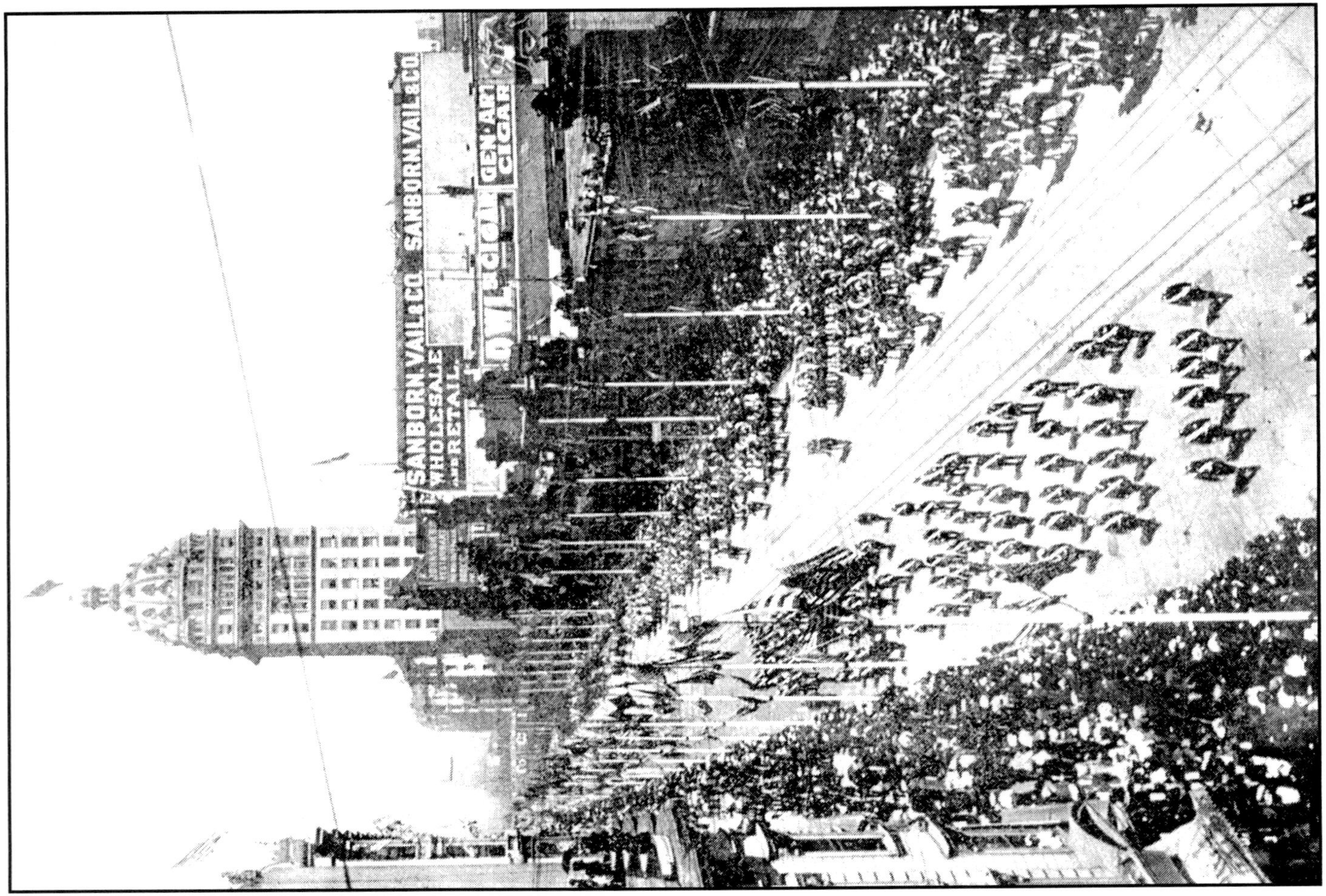

Looking down Market Street during Knights Templars Parade, 1904.

The Business District of San Francisco Burning, as Seen from Fairmont Hotel.

The Palace Hotel before the Fire.

Palace Hotel, San Francisco, after the Fire, with Monadnock Block on right. Walls withstood both Fire and Earthquake.

Bread Line on Folsom Street, San Francisco.

Sacramento and Franklin Streets, where the Fire was Checked.

Capp Street, near Seventeenth, Damaged by Earthquake.

Cottages on Golden Gate Avenue, near Hyde Street, Wrecked by Earthquake.

Looking down Sutter Street, San Francisco, after the Fire.

The James Flood Building after the Fire. Building was gutted by the Fire, but apparently not otherwise damaged. The City Treasurer then had his office here together with Western National Bank.

The Result of the Earthquake on the block between Seventeenth and Eighteenth, looking North on Howard Street.

California Theatre, Bush Street, near Kearny.

Union Square, Hotel St. Francis, and Dewey Monument after the Fire.

Temporary Hotel St. Francis, built in Union Square after the Fire.

People fleeing from the flames resting in Union Square. All Buildings shown here afterwards burned.

Looking down Fell Street. Showing how closely people clung to their homes, only leaving when fire was a few doors away.

Grace Church, on California and Stockton Streets.

The Burning of the Emporium. All the Buildings shown here were destroyed by Fire.

United States Custom House, corner Sansome and Washington Streets, withstood Fire and Earthquake.

The Call Building, seen through a tangle of ruins.

Museum, Golden Gate Park. Damaged by Earthquake.

Looking North on Kearny Street, from Post, after the Fire.

Montgomery Street, looking North from California Street.

Montgomery Street, looking South from California Street.

Residences of Messrs. Flood, Huntington and Crocker before the Fire.

The ruins of the Crocker and Flood Palatial Residences. These Residences with their Magnificent Furnishings and Art Treasures represent a loss of Millions.

The Music Stand, Golden Gate Park, Damaged by Earthquake.

The Burning City, seen from the Bay the morning of April 18, 1906.

The Break in the Street on Van Ness Avenue, near Vallejo Street, caused by Earthquake. Water Mains broken here.

The Burning of the Call Building, as seen from Kearny Street. The Mutual Savings Bank Building in the foreground.

Home of Clau Spreckels, where Fire was checked, on Van Ness Avenue, corner Clay Street.

St. Dominic's Church, Bush and Steiner Streets—Wrecked by Earthquake.

St. Ignatius Church, Hayes Street and Van Ness Avenue.

Ruins of Chinatown District.

Repairing Tracks on Sutter Street after the Fire. Changing Line from Cable to Electric.

Montgomery Block, corner Montgomery and Washington Streets—Escaped Fire though all other Buildings were Burned in same Block.

Old Mission Dolores—Unhurt by Earthquake or Fire.

Ruins of Hibernia Bank Building and Prager's Department Store—Jones, McAllister and Market Streets.

Van Ness Avenue, the New Business Street, looking from Geary Street North, December, 1906.

A portion of the City not damaged by either Fire or Earthquake—Looking East from Alta Plaza.

Scottish Rite, Masonic Hall, with Jewish Synagogue on the left, Geary Street, near Fillmore, San Francisco, Damaged by Earthquake.

Sunset District, looking from Ashbury Heights—Unharmed by Fire or Earthquake.

Looking South from Alta Plaza—A portion of Residence Section which escaped Fire.

In foreground is the first "Class A: Fireproof Building built since the Fire, with the Mutual Savings Bank Building behind it, which was one of the first to be repaired and occupied.

Rebuilding San Francisco—Laying Foundation for Fireproof Building at California and Market Street.

Showing the Four Blocks from Sixteenth to Twentieth Streets Rebuilt Since the Fire. Taken November, 1906.

The New Loop at the Ferry for Car Service. Completed November, 1906.

North side Market Street, between Jones and Larkin, Rebuilt since Fire. From photograph taken November, 1906.

Some New Buildings on Fillmore Street, the Principal Business Center, Immediately after the Fire.

Stanford Library, Stanford University—Damaged by Earthquake.

View showing a portion of the Asylum for the Insane at Agnews. Wrecked by Earthquake.

Another portion of the Wrecked Asylum by Agnews, showing Results of Earthquake.

Sonoma County Courthouse, Santa Rosa, before the Earthquake.

Sonoma County Courthouse, Santa Rosa, after the Earthquake.

Wells Fargo Bank Building, Santa Rosa, Destroyed by Earthquake.

Colophon

This book has been set in Caxton, a *Garalde* typeface. Designed by Leslie Usherwood in 1981 for Letraset, it is of an old style design, with a large x-height (small case letters.) Having short serifs and high-waisted capitals, it is a text face intended for use in journals and books. The design makes it easy to read in small point sizes.

The typestyle is named for William Caxton, an early printer and the first person to publish in English, while he was in the Netherlands during 1471. He is primarily known for publishing Chaucer's *Canterbury Tales* in England.

The title font is Templar, a victorian typestyle found in books and newspapers of the time.

Back Cover Illustration: A panorama of burned downtown San Francisco.